HOW TO WRITE
LETTERS

CELIA WARREN

QED Publishing

First published in the UK in 2007 by
QED Publishing
A Quarto Group company
226 City Road
London EC1V 2TT
www.qed-publishing.co.uk

A Catalogue record for this book is available from the British Library.

ISBN 978 1 84538 904 8

Written by Celia Warren
Designed by Jackie Palmer
Editor Louisa Somerville
Illustrations by Tim Loughead
Consultant Anne Faundez

Publisher Steve Evans
Creative Director Zeta Davies
Senior Editor Hannah Ray

Printed and bound in China

CONTENTS

ALL KINDS OF LETTERS

Ever since writing was invented, people have communicated through letters and other kinds of written messages. With the arrival of electronic mail (**email**), we still spend much of our time sending each other written messages. Here are some examples of ways we communicate in writing.

Informal letter

If you write to someone you know well, you can use a chatty **tone**, as if you can hear your voice talking to the other person. This is suitable for a catching-up, newsy letter to a friend or a thank-you letter to a relative.

Tip
Put 'regards', 'kind regards' or 'best wishes' instead of 'love from' if it's someone you don't know that well.

Dear Susy,
It was great to see you on Sunday...

...and they would love to meet up again soon.

With love from

Always start with 'dear' – or even 'darling' if it's someone you know very well!

*Use a **comma** after the person's name.*

Postcard

It's usual only to send postcards to good friends, family and neighbours, so they will be quite **informal**. There's a picture on one side and your message and the address of the **recipient** has to fit on the other. There's not much room, then! You will need to keep your handwriting small or not say much.

Having a fab time here in the mountains. Our hotel is just across a wooden bridge. It's really comfy but there's no TV. I don't really mind 'cos there's loads of things to do. Climbed up to the top of Craggy Hill today and paddled in a stream on the way down. Food's great. Weather's brill.
See you soon. Love, Carl.

*You can leave out the **greeting** to save space and jump straight in with the message.*

*Use **abbreviations** to save space.*

Formal letter

When you write to someone who you don't know that well, you don't want to write a chatty letter. You should use a more **formal** style.

Dear Mrs Dusty,
I really enjoyed my visit to the Museum of...

Yours sincerely,

*The closing **phrase** is separated from your **signature** by a comma.*

Tip
In formal letters, start with
- Dear Sir (to a man)
- Dear Madam (to a woman)
- Dear Sir or Madam (if you don't know which, and can't find out)

Very formal letter

Sometimes you may need to write to someone whose name you don't know or choose not to use.

The name of the recipient and/or their job title comes first.

The Director
Stuffwells Taxidermists

Dear Sir,
I would like to find out about the services that you offer and...

Yours faithfully,

Put the name of the company above the greeting.

Tip
When you write 'Dear Sir' or 'Dear Madam' use the ending 'Yours faithfully'.

Email

The fastest way to communicate in writing is by email. You send a letter typed on your computer keyboard to the computer of the recipient. They can then open your email and read your words on their screen. You can also send attachments (word files or pictures) tagged onto your email for the reader to open and look at.

People tend to start emails with 'Hi', especially to friends and family.

Subject: HOW R U?
From: Jade Jones < j.jones@urserver.com
To: Susie Smith < s.smith@supersupplier.co.uk
Hi Susie,
Just deleting old mails and reread yours. Sorry I never replied – been soooo busy! How's things? Have you heard from Jack? I saw him last week at the rock festival. Took funny pic (see attached jpeg).
See ya!
Jade

Shortened words and incomplete sentences are fine.

LAYING OUT LETTERS

Whether you are writing an informal letter or a formal one, there are different ways of laying out your letter, so that it is easy to read.

Tip

Put a sheet of ruled paper underneath your plain paper as a guide to keep your writing in straight lines. It looks better than writing on ruled paper.

Informal letter to a grandparent

The date goes on the left above your greeting.

Write your address in the top right-hand corner of the page.

22 Stables End,
ROCKINGTON
Shrubshire
TN80 4QT

17th January 2007

Dear Grandad,

Thank you so much for the money you sent me for my birthday. I'm going to spend it on...

Love from
Jon

*If you have paper with a **letterhead**, you only need to put the date before starting your letter.*

The Spinney
Long Lane
FAIRFORDHILL-ON-SEA

17th January 2007

Dear...

Springboard

Use one of the following addresses as inspiration for who you are, where you live and what you are writing about. Create a suitable name for yourself and for the person you are writing to. Make sure you lay out your letter in an appropriate **format**.

Highwire House
Juggler's Lane
Custardswell
Slopshire

Cutlass Cottage
Jolly Roger Road
Walkwell-on-Plank
Cornwall

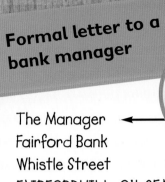

Formal letter to a bank manager

Write the recipient's address at the top left of the page.

The Manager
Fairford Bank
Whistle Street
FAIRFORDHILL-ON-SEA

The Spinney
Long Lane
FAIRFORDHILL-ON-SEA

Put your own address at the top right of the page.

13th April 2007

Don't forget the date!

Dear Madam,

*After 'Dear Sir/Madam', you may want to state the **subject** of your letter before starting to write it. In this case, it is usual to centre your subject. You could write in capital letters and underline it to make it stand out.*

OPENING A YOUNG SAVER'S ACCOUNT

I am interested in learning more about your YSA scheme as advertised in this week's *Fairford Gazette*. Please could you send me an application form at the above address.

Yours faithfully,

Molly Beer

Molly Beer

*SAE enclosed

When you address an envelope, start halfway down the envelope and left of centre. Begin each line of the address directly under the one above.

*SAE

SAE stands for 'stamped addressed envelope'. Including an envelope that is stamped and addressed to yourself encourages the recipient to reply to your letter at no cost to themselves. It is polite if you are asking someone for a reply or for them to send you something.

Molly Beer
The Spinney
Long Lane
FAIRFORDHILL-ON-SEA

Tip

Do not put an SAE into a chatty letter to a friend. If they intend to reply, they will happily pay their own postage as you are their friend. If you include an SAE to them they will probably be either offended, or feel pressured into writing – or both!

FINDING YOUR VOICE

When you write a letter, it is important to write clearly so that what you say will be understood. You don't have your voice or facial expressions to convey your message. As you write your letter, picture the person who will be reading it. Imagine how they will react to your words. From your opening line you set the tone of your letter. Make sure you continue to the end in the same 'voice' as you started.

Misunderstandings

When words are spoken face to face, the listener can **see** your eyes, and the expression on your face and judge your intention. If you say something that they misunderstand, you can correct your words straight away.

In a letter, the recipient can only judge what you are saying by the words you have written. They might misunderstand what you are saying. This is especially so in the case of jokes. Make sure you joke only to people who know you very well and understand your sense of humour. Otherwise they might not realize that you're joking and could be upset.

Tip

Re-read your letter before posting it, to make sure everything is clear. You could even **role-play** your reader's reaction when they open the letter, to help you to adopt their viewpoint.

If you are writing a formal letter to someone you don't know:

- Begin with 'Dear Sir' or 'Dear Mr Smith' (or 'Dear Madam' / 'Dear Mrs Smith').
- Use phrases, such as 'I would' and 'Please could you'.
- Don't use contractions, such as 'I'm' and 'won't'.
- Don't use slang words, such as 'fab'.
- End your letter with 'Yours faithfully' or 'Yours sincerely'.

If you write a chatty letter to a friend:

- Use their name or nickname, such as 'Dear Mo'.
- Use contractions, such as 'I've' and 'shouldn't'.
- Use lots of adjectives, such as 'cool' and 'fantastic'.
- End your letter with 'Love from...'.
- Don't forget to add some kisses!

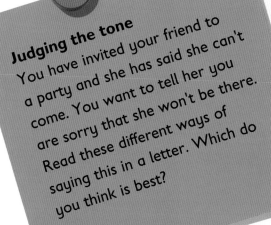

Judging the tone

You have invited your friend to a party and she has said she can't come. You want to tell her you are sorry that she won't be there. Read these different ways of saying this in a letter. Which do you think is best?

A

I do think it's a shame you won't be at my party. I really wanted you there. You will miss all the fun.

B

I am disappointed you can't make my party. It won't be the same without you there.

C

What a shame you can't make it to my party. I understand why you can't come but I'll miss you. Let's get together next week and I can tell you all about it.

A. Sounds a bit moody and self-centred – the first two sentences both start with 'I'. She might think that you didn't understand that she really wanted to come to the party, but couldn't. This letter might make her feel guilty, which would be unfair as she was sad to miss the party.

B. Sounds a bit better than A. But the reader might think you are disappointed in her personally, rather than disappointed not to be seeing her at the party.

C. Sounds best of the three. It focuses on the reader rather than the writer. It suggests sympathy and understanding rather than blame. It also ends on a positive note, suggesting a fresh opportunity to meet.

Springboard

Pretend to be the party-thrower and try finishing off letter option C. (Begin the letter with 'Dear...'.)

THANK-YOU LETTERS

Thank-you letters can be very easy or really hard to write. A lot can depend on the following factors:

- What are you saying thank you for: a kind deed, a thoughtful present or a party you went to?
- How well do you know the generous person – very well, a little, or not at all?
- Did you expect the present or help, or was it a surprise?
- Did you like the present or party?
- Are you writing for yourself or on behalf of a group of people?

Being polite

What if Aunt Julie sent a present you hate – something too young or too small for you: an ugly doll with purple hair, a set of bath toys or a hideous sweater? How can you be polite about it?

Tip

Find something positive to say, however loosely linked to the present. For example:

- What a surprise those bath toys were! Mum will expect me to wash now – it's not natural!

- Thank you for that lovely top. My favourite colour! It must have taken you years to knit.

- Many thanks for the doll. I had fun choosing a name and decided in the end that Maxi will suit her best.

ACTIVITY

Try writing a thank-you letter on behalf of your class to a theatre group that recently visited your school. Things for you to think about include:

- What did they perform? What was special about their act?
- Did your class join in? If so, how?
- How did you and your friends react and respond?
- Would you like them to come again some time?

Begin:

Dear Actors,

I am writing on behalf of Class... following your visit to our school last week...

Springboard

Write a thank you letter for a strange present whose purpose you can't work out!

WORDS TO HELP YOU: fascinating, intriguing, interesting, unusual, fun

Thanking strangers

It might seem odd to write and say 'thank you' for a present to someone you don't know, but it can happen. Mums and dads have lots of friends. Perhaps one of them met you when you were a baby and still sends you a present each year. You don't know the person but you have to say 'thank you'. What can you write about?

Tell the reader the purpose of the letter.

Give reasons why she made an especially good choice. Phrasing the first reason as a question sounds friendly – as if you were talking to her.

Shows you know who she is and suggests you are interested in her, not just her gift.

Offer something interesting for her to think about: a glimpse of what is happening in your life. The scarf gets another mention – not essential, but an added bonus!

Informal closing words are more friendly than 'yours sincerely'.

The letters 'PS' stand for postscript (Latin for 'after writing') – useful for adding afterthoughts, separating them from the letter's main purpose.

13th April 2007

Dear Aunt Julie,

I am writing to thank you for the lovely scarf you sent for my birthday. Did you know yellow is my favourite colour? It's so warm and arrived in perfect time. I wore it when I went ice-skating with my friends last week.

Mum tells me you used to go ice-skating with her when you were my age. I wonder if you fell over as often as I did? Probably not – who could beat my record?

Next week we go back to school. I'll be in a new class with a new teacher. Everyone who was in her class last year calls her The Dragon. I hope my scarf has protective powers that save people from dragons!

Hope you are well and having fun.

With very best wishes,

Dale

PS Mum sends her love.

LETTER TO A PENFRIEND

A penfriend is usually someone you have never met. They live in another part of the country – maybe even the other side of the world. Or perhaps it is someone you met on holiday and you both decided to keep in touch. If English is not their first language, keep the language that you use when you write simple.

Tip

You don't want your letter to read like a page from a diary. Nor do you want it to read like an **autobiography** – 'My Life So Far'! Avoid beginning every sentence with 'I' (though it's fine to include a handful!).

Why write?

You are writing to each other to make friends. You could share information about:

- yourself, your home and family – any pets
- your school and home town
- your hobbies and interests
- what kinds of music and films you like

11th June 2007

11 Bruton Street, Wingford TT4 9BG

Dear Carlos,

My name is Jake and I'm 11 years old. My sister, Molly, is two years older than me. She has a pet guinea pig and I have two rats, called Tricky and Nibbles. Sometimes we let them play together and they get on really well. Do you have any pets?

My best friend is called George. We both have games consoles so we can play together after school. ICT is my favourite subject at school. It's cool! I also like writing, which is why I wanted a penfriend. What's your best subject?

Tomorrow I'm going to the ten-screen cinema to see a new sci-fi film. I'll tell you all about it next time I write.

Hope to hear from you soon. Please tell me all about life in Spain!

Your new friend,

Jake

You want to learn the same sort of information about them, in the hope that you have things in common, shared interests, and will get on well.

ACTIVITY

Find out if your town is twinned with a town in another country. Write to a new penfriend from your twin town. Include information about your town and local environment in your letter. Ask a few questions about your penfriend, for him or her to answer.

Tips on finding a penfriend

• If your school has links with a school in another part of the country or abroad they may be able to help you find a friend to write to.

• If your home town is twinned with a town abroad, the Twinning Association may find you a penfriend.

• Write a letter to your favourite comic or magazine asking if another reader would like to **correspond** with you. (The magazine should not publish your address, but send on any **responses** to you.)

Signing off

You can't write 'Love from…' when you don't know somebody very well. 'Best wishes', 'All the best' or 'Regards' are all fine. You are opening doors to friendship without assuming you will be great pals too soon. When you first write to a new penfriend you will need to include your surname as you sign off. You don't need to include it in subsequent letters.

Springboard

Imagine that another planet has recently been twinned with Earth. Write a letter from an alien who lives on the twin planet. Write as if you were that alien, telling your human reader all about yourself and your planet. You might even enclose a recent 'school photo' of yourself!

LETTERS TO OFFICIALS

One reason that people write letters is to express an **opinion** in public, but why do people put their feelings into writing? And where do they send their letters?

TO TRY TO MAKE SOMETHING HAPPEN

Reasons for writing

You may want to write an official letter for one or more of these reasons:

TO HIGHLIGHT A PROBLEM, SUCH AS A SAFETY ISSUE

TO TRY TO PREVENT SOMETHING HAPPENING

TO COMPLAIN

Sending it off

When you write to express an opinion, you hope that someone will take notice and act upon what you have to say. This means it is important to send your letter to the correct person. It's no good complaining to the council about getting too much homework; they can't do anything about it! Don't write to your headteacher to complain about the cinema closing. It's nothing to do with her!

Tip

If you cannot find out whom to write to, perhaps the editor of the local paper will know. You could always write to the paper with your concern, in the hope that they might print your letter.

ACTIVITY

Imagine that your local council plans to close the play area in your local park and turn it into a golf course. With a group of friends, write a series of letters to the council and / or the editor of the local paper about the golf course proposal. Adopt the points of view of different members of the local community, such as:

- Local golfers. They think it's great – or most do. Some say they won't be able to afford the higher proposed membership fees.
- The local wildlife society. It is not happy. Its members say that rare insects and birds will suffer if the trees are cut down.

Remember that these will be formal letters, so begin 'Dear Sir/Madam' and finish 'Yours faithfully...'

Springboard

Write a letter to a celebrity asking them to visit your friend who has been in hospital for a long time. Explain why you chose them, how their visit will speed your friend's recovery and why they deserve a visit. This time, instead of 'Dear Sir/Madam', use the celebrity's name. End with 'Yours sincerely'.

Present the situation.

Express your opinion, explaining briefly why you hold your view.

Make a suggestion.

Request some specific action – including a reply to your letter.

23 Greendale View
Jobsworth

Jobsworth District Council
Jobsworth

16th June 2007

Dear Councillor Brown,

<u>TOWN PLANNING APPLICATION</u>

I am really worried about the plan to turn my local leisure park into a private golf club. I am a ten year-old who plays there regularly and I don't want this to happen.

My brother and I and all our friends have played there all our lives, as did my mum and dad when they were children. We also have swimming lessons and clubs at the swimming pool.

If the park and pool close we will have nowhere safe to play. The nearest swimming pool is ten miles away. For our safety, we must learn to swim because there are rivers and a reservoir nearby.

Golf players are mostly grown-ups who can drive out of town to play golf. Why don't you use wasteland where there would be plenty of room for an 18-hole golf course, and leave the rest of us to enjoy the park and swimming pool, and keep fit and safe?

Please take my suggestions seriously and talk about them at your next meeting. Please write and let me know what you're going to do.

Yours sincerely,

Make sure your whole letter fits on one side of a sheet of paper.

DRAFTING A REPLY

Sometimes you will receive a letter that needs a reply. It is often best to **draft** your letter first before you send it. Read this letter and think about how you might respond.

Dear Reader,

SPECIALIST ADVENTURE HOLIDAYS

Are you aged between 7 and 13?

Do you like challenging fun and adventure?

Have you ever wanted to learn new skills and test them to the limit?

Would you love to make new friends in an exciting environment?

If the answer to all these is YES, then you could enjoy a Specialist Adventure Holiday in a beautiful region of lakes and mountains with like-minded people of your own age.

We are offering ONE FREE PLACE on this holiday of a lifetime. If you would like to be considered, write and tell us what strengths you would bring to the experience and what you would hope to gain from the fortnight's fun. Also tell us which outdoor event you would most like to try and why: kayaking, caving, archery, white-water canoeing, mountaineering, sailing.

Write to Harry Bold at:

Specialist Adventure Holidays
PO Box 12
The Lake District

I look forward to hearing from you.

Yours sincerely,

Jane Gray

PP Harry Bold

The letters 'pp' stand for 'per persona' (Latin for 'for the person'). They are used when someone signs a letter on behalf of another person, in their absence.

- Write your own address and the recipient's in the correct places.
- Where will you put the date?
- Decide whether to write 'Dear Mr Bold', using his **title**, or 'Dear Harry'. What different effect will each choice have?
- Start a new paragraph for each part of your letter.

Springboard

Draft a reply to one of these letters that you have received through the post:
- A request from your favourite pop star asking you to join their band.
- A letter from your best friend who has moved to Australia.
- A letter from an alien inviting you to visit planet Zog.

---

22 Dog Lane
Whippet-on-the-Wold
Lincolnshire

Specialist Adventure Holidays
PO Box 12
The Lake District

7th June

Dear Mr Bold,

I picked up a copy of your letter at a local leisure centre, and I am writing in the hope of winning a place on a Specialist Adventure Holiday this summer.

As an active ten year-old, I like lots of sports. Recently, I gained my bronze life-saving swimming certificate and would love to try scuba diving and canoeing.

I've always wanted to visit the Lake District, so I hope you will consider offering me a place. My teacher says I'd be good at kayaking but I can't afford classes. This holiday would provide me with the perfect opportunity to learn.

I do hope I have convinced you of my enthusiasm and look forward to hearing from you.

Yours sincerely,
Sam Smith

When you have written your draft, read it aloud.

- Are your sentences short and to the point? If you run out of breath reading a sentence, then it is too long. Break it up into two shorter sentences.

- Does your letter fit on one side of paper? If not, then find ways to shorten it. Cut out any waffle. Make sure you haven't said the same thing twice in different ways.

- Sum up what you have said in your final paragraph to remind Harry Bold of what has gone before.

SENDING POSTCARDS

People often send postcards to friends and relations when they go on holiday. But you don't have to be on holiday to send a postcard. You might send one to a friend to show them the town or area where you live. Postcards are also a useful way of keeping in touch or sending a short message.

Unique message

What you write on the back of a postcard makes it more interesting and personalizes it. As there is not much space on a postcard, it's often best to leave out a greeting. The name and address alongside make it clear to whom you are writing. Mostly, you can pitch straight in with your message: 'Wish you were here'? No, there must be something better than that!

Tip

When you send holiday postcards you can usually write more or less the same message on each one. However, if you are sending a postcard to two friends or relatives who will compare cards, remember to choose different pictures and think of new things to write on each card.

You could tell your friends about:
- a fascinating fact that you've learnt about the place where you are staying
- what you did yesterday
- what you hope to do tomorrow
- how you find the local people and their customs
- if you have had a chance to practise a foreign language
- what the food and accommodation are like and – if you must – what the weather's like!

As space is limited, you can miss out a few words, such as 'the' and 'I' – the reader is clever enough to work those out for themselves!

Paragraphs can be ignored, too.

Staying in a wicked hotel! It's got everything: pool tables, jacuzzi, sauna, pool – the lot! Tomorrow, going climbing on sheer rock-face – can't wait! They provide safety gear so I'll see you back at school next term, no worries!
Bye for now,
Charlie

Mr Simon Pomfrey
56a City Heights
BURNINGTON
BU8 5QT

ACTIVITY

Try designing your own postcards. Here are some ways you can make them:

- Draw and colour a picture on a rectangle of white card about 15 x 10cm. It can be a picture of anything; your pet, a place that you love or your house. Cover it with clear, adhesive film. On the other side of the card draw a line down the middle, a rectangle where the stamp goes and lines for the address, Add a title for the picture at the bottom.

- Design your postcards on a computer and print them out. You could use digital photographs of yourself or your friends and family, or photos of scenery. You could divide the postcard into quarters with a circle in the centre, and put a different photograph – or Clip Art – in each section.

- Make a collage from things you have collected from your holiday: cut-outs from photos or brochures, tickets, menus, pressed leaves and flowers. Stick them onto a rectangle of card and cover with clear, adhesive film.

Tropical sunset, Bali

glue stick

Springboard

Buy or make a postcard to send to someone who lives alone and may not get much post – for example, a grandparent who lives far away, a great aunt or uncle. You could even send it to a neighbour as a cheery surprise!

19

FANTASY LETTERS

You have learned a lot about writing letters. How about writing some in a fantasy situation? You can role-play, writing in the **persona** of a fantasy character or a character who, in real life, could not write the letter for themselves.

Here are some suggestions:

• Write a letter from one fantasy character to another

It could be a mermaid writing to Santa Claus, explaining about the absence of a chimney or Santa Claus writing to the mermaid to apologize for the socks he gave her last year (not much use if you have a tail!).

• Write the letter you wrote and never sent

Perhaps you wanted to have a moan to someone about something but in the end you decided it would hurt their feelings too much to send it to them. Or maybe you were writing to decline the invitation to be bridesmaid or page boy at your aunt's wedding, but decided you could cope with wearing a silly, frilly dress or shirt for a few hours, after all. Have fun writing the letter... but don't send it!

• Write a letter from a pet to its owner

Maybe the pet is complaining about its living conditions or its lifestyle. For example: you could pretend to be a hamster who complains that his wheel squeaks and he needs his cage cleaning more often; a guinea pig who complains about her diet (her carrots are soft and she would like some celery for a change); a dog who requests some new places to go 'walkies' with more lampposts and new smells – he's bored with the old ones.

• Write the letter you were never meant to see

You have found a letter which no-one intended you should ever read. Why? Perhaps it holds some dark secret about your ancestors – were they highwaymen? Or is it some other family secret? Or is it a pair of love-letters between your mother and father long before you were born, sounding all soppy and nothing like them!

ACTIVITY

When you have finished, try writing some letters of reply.

If you enjoy writing stories as well as letters you could combine the two. Have a go at telling a story through an exchange of letters between two characters. Any other characters in the story will only be made known to the reader through what the two correspondents say about them.

Ask an adult to help you to melt candlewax to make a seal for the envelope.

Dearest Ma,

I be writing this note by candlelight as since I surprised that latest coach on the high road, not a mile from your cottage, I dare not show my face by day. It's not for nowt that they call your son The Second Dick Turpin!

Should anything happen to me afore we meet, your future is secure. The Third Oak holds some rewards three foot West of its trunk. Let it not be said that I let my dear Ma go hungry.

Do not expect me by day but if a masked man taps upon your window in the small hours, I beg you grant him access. It will be I, your own loving son,

Tom

You could try writing the letter in ink with a quill pen made from a feather.

To make the paper look old, add some tea stains. Ask an adult to brown your letter in a hot oven for a few minutes.

WRITING IN CODE

Ever since people learned to read and write, letters that needed to be kept secret have been written in code. Some codes are easier to crack than others. Here are some examples:

Codes that involve rearranging the layout of the lettering:

ACTIVITY

Try using one of these codes or make up a new one with a friend. To invent a letter code, write out the alphabet across or down a piece of paper. Then write your code letters or numbers beside each original letter. Now you can send each other messages to decode.

Earj ohni hopey oua rew elln. Extw eeki amh avingap artyw. Illy oub ea blet oc omed?

Dear John, I hope you are well. Next week I am having a party. Will you be able to come?

Dea rjo hni hop eyo uar ewe llN ext wee kia mha vin gap art yWi lly oub eab let oco me?

Dear John, I hope you are well. Next week I am having a party. Will you be able to come?

Here, in each sentence, the first letter of each word hops onto the end of the word before.

Raed nhoj I epoh uoy era llew. Txen keew I ma gnivah a ytrap. Lliw uoy eb elba ot emoc?

Dear John, I hope you are well. Next week I am having a party. Will you be able to come?

Here every word has three letters – but it is the same message as before. A capital letter shows when a new sentence starts.

Again, this is saying the same, but here each word is spelled backwards.

Codes that involve reading some words and not others – every third word, for example:

Bananas are dear today so Leah and I please will not meet up soon. Joe is not at home for the week. Oh well!

Dear Leah, Please meet Joe at the well.

Tip

Single-letter words speed up cracking a code, so join 'I' and 'a' up to other words to make your code harder to crack.

Coded messages that can be read in the mirror:

Dear Leah, Please meet Joe at the well.

Dear Leah, Please meet Joe at the well.

A code that substitutes the next letter in the alphabet to represent each letter of the original message:

• EFBS MFBI QMFBTF NFFU KPF BU UIF XFMM

Dear Leah, Please meet Joe at the well.

Tip

If you use numbers for your code, don't use them in order A=1, B=2, and so on. That's too easy to crack.

Springboard

Create a **pseudonym** to conceal your identity. See if you can think one up that gives clues as to who you are really, such as an anagram of your name. For example, ALICE WARNER could sign herself RARE LAWN ICE.

HINT: To form an anagram, write the letters of your name on separate slips of paper. Jumble them up and see what new name you can create.

Or you could try combining your pet's name with a pop star, such as FIDO DIDO.

SUMMING UP

Here are some final points to think about when writing a letter.

1. Picture the person you are writing to as you write.

2. In an informal letter, write as you would speak – don't try to use sophisticated language just because it is written down.

3. Draft your letter first on scrap paper. Then you can concentrate fully on neat, legible handwriting for the **fair copy**.

4. Plan how to fold your letter so that it fits in the envelope. Practise with a spare piece first.

5. Always remember to date your letter – including the year.

6. Keep your sentences short and read them aloud to check they make sense.

7. Remember, if your letter begins 'Dear Sir' (or Madam), then it must end 'Yours faithfully'.

8. Keep letters to recipients other than your friends to one side of the paper.

9. Avoid starting every sentence with 'I…'.

10. Stop and think twice before pressing 'Send' on an email.

Here are some further suggestions for practising your letter-writing skills. Write a letter to:

- a child of the future – perhaps your great-great-grandchild who is not yet born

- the grandfather or grandmother who you never met

- a famous historical character, such as Abraham Lincoln or Florence Nightingale

- your favourite fictional character

- your future self. Seal and address the envelope and write at the top: NOT TO BE OPENED UNTIL YOUR 21ST BIRTHDAY

Imagine you have just moved house. You are missing your old home and friends. Write your first email to your best friend. You want to sound upbeat and positive, and tell them all about your new home and locality. At the same time, you want them to know you think about them a lot. Try to strike a happy balance as you draft your email.

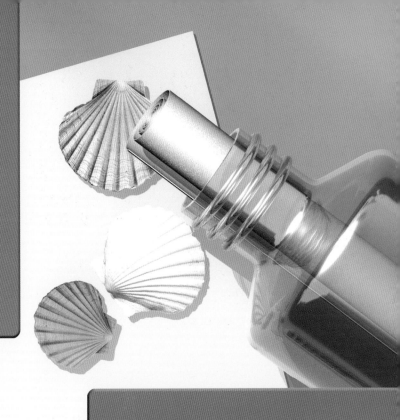

Imagine you are stranded on a desert island surrounded by sea. All you have is writing materials. A bottle floats ashore. You write a letter, seal it in the bottle and throw it out to sea in the hope that someone will find and read it. What will you say in your 'Dear Anybody...' letter?

Laura's room
Upstairs at No 5

June 5th
Dear Mrs Collins,
    Would you like to join me for tea this afternoon? Please RSVP by lunchtime.

Yours sincerely,

Laura

Write a letter to a member of your family in a formal style, as if you didn't know them well. For example:

• A thank-you letter to Dad for cooking dinner (beginning Dear Mr...).

• A letter to your brother or sister requesting a tour of their room (beginning Dear Mr / Miss).

• An invitation to Mum to join you for tea.

GLOSSARY

Abbreviation shortened word, such as Rd for road; Dr for doctor

Autobiography a book written by someone about their own life

BCC blind carbon copy – a secret copy of a letter sent to another person. Often used when sending emails.

CC carbon copy – an identical copy of a letter or email sent to another person

Comma a punctuation mark, used to show a pause

Correspond to exchange letters or emails

Correspondent a person with whom you exchange letters or emails

Draft a first, rough version of a letter, to be checked and improved.

Email short for electronic mail

Fair copy correct final copy of a letter that is ready to be sent

Formal following conventional rules and using correct language

Format style, such as the layout of a letter on the page

Greeting the opening phrase of a letter (eg. 'Dear...')

Informal relaxed and casual, easy style

Letterhead address printed at the top of a letter

Opinion a personal point of view (rather than a fact)

Paragraph one or more sentences on a subject, beginning on a new line

Persona character or identity

Phrase a group of words

pp per persona – meaning 'on behalf of'. Used when a letter is signed on behalf of someone who is not there

PS post script – meaning 'after writing'. Text following the main writing and after the signature. Useful for afterthoughts.

Pseudonym a false name or 'pen name' used by a writer

Recipient a person who receives (say, a letter)

Response a reply

Role-play behaving as if you were another person

RSVP répondez s'il vous plait – meaning 'please reply'

Signature someone's name, handwritten by themselves

Statement an account of facts, rather than opinions

Subject what you are writing about

Tone your style of writing, which could be chatty (if you are writing to a friend) or more formal

Text written words

Title a person's status that appears before their name, such as Mr, Mrs, Miss, Ms, Sir, Lady, Doctor, Professor, Reverend

INDEX

PARENT AND TEACHER NOTES

- It is not for nothing that people talk of letter-writing as an 'art' — one that is practised less and less in these days of emails and text messaging. All of these forms of correspondence are part of the same basic human need to communicate with others. Correspondence, whether formal or informal, instant or considered, is explored broadly in this book. Every page informs and teaches, while encouraging children to put pen to paper or fingers to keyboard.

- Some children will be familiar with terms, such as 'PS' and 'RSVP' but may not know their meaning. The glossary on page 30 includes abbreviations of terms that are useful in letter-writing.

- There is much scope for the imagination and for creative writing in pretend letters. The more your child gets pleasure from writing letters for fun, the easier it becomes and writing letters 'for real' becomes less of a chore.

- Encourage your child to show an interest in letter-writing that stretches beyond writing pretend letters for fun. It would be beneficial if your child could go one step further and send real letters to real people and experience the pleasure of receiving a posted reply.

- Your child could write, for example, to a company requesting information or a catalogue. This will show your child how writing a letter can bring a result. They might write to the letters page of a children's magazine — and possibly see their letter in print.

- Help your child to improve their letter-writing. Knowing how to draft and re-draft letters — especially formal ones — will help them throughout their life.

- Many of the ground rules for letter-writing presented in this book will stand your child in good stead in later years when they need to apply in writing for a job or a place on a study course.

- You can help your child by providing paper and envelopes. Attractive notelets or postcards will help to make the writing of thank-you letters a pleasure instead of a chore.

- Help younger children to check that the envelope is the right way up before they write the address, provide stamps for them to post real letters or, perhaps, write back to them if they write to you for fun.

- Perhaps you could provide your child with an address book and help them to add names and addresses alphabetically to encourage them to write letters to friends and relations.